# CRITICAL THINKING ACTIVITIES FOR KIDS

ILLUSTRATED BY SR. RENY

# Critical THINKING

## ACTiVITIES FoR KiDS

### Fun and Challenging Games to Boost Brain Power

TAYLOR LANG, M.Ed.

CALLISTO PUBLISHING

*To the Summit Sparks and Tyler Run Tigers, for helping me learn how to teach thinking, and to my parents, for always encouraging me to go the extra mile!*

Published by Callisto Publishing LLC C/O Sourcebooks LLC
P.O. Box 4410, Naperville, Illinois 60567-4410
(630) 961-3900
callistopublishing.com

This product conforms to all applicable CPSC and CPSIA standards.

Source of Production: 1010 Printing Asia Limited, Kwun Tong, Hong Kong, China
Date of Production: September 2023
Run Number: 5033989

Printed and bound in China.
OGP 10 9

# Contents

# Introduction
## FOR PARENTS AND TEACHERS

**Hello there!**

It's wonderful you've chosen to help your child discover the power of critical thinking. Kids who build strategic thinking skills from a young age become increasingly curious about the world around them and evolve into lifelong learners. As an experienced classroom teacher, I've seen firsthand how the development of strong critical thinking skills leads to academic success. I hope this book serves as a tool to help you help your child learn *how* to think, while having fun along the way!

## WHAT IS CRITICAL THINKING?

From creating a grocery list to casting a ballot in an election, critical thinking skills are the foundation of many aspects of our everyday lives. Whenever we take in pieces of information and mentally comb through them to determine what we should do next, we engage in critical thinking. As adults, we identify problems, draw comparisons, make judgments, and execute decisions multiple times in an hour without thinking about all the cognitive processes involved.

When children combine new information with their background knowledge and experiences, they can:

- Explain why something happens. (I can see that *x* caused *y* to occur; I know that *y* is a result of *x*'s happening.)

- Compare and contrast items. (How is something similar to something else? How does it differ?)

- Evaluate ideas. (Is this idea possible or ridiculous?)

- Form opinions. (I prefer *x* over *y* because . . . )

- Understand other people's viewpoints. (Even if I don't agree, I see what you are saying.)

- Predict what may happen in the future. (Based on these events, I believe _____ will happen.)

- Solve problems with creative solutions

This book focuses on six essential critical thinking skills. The skills taught through the activities are:

**IDENTIFYING:** making distinctions between multiple things

**ANALYZING:** figuring out how one thing relates to another

**REASONING:** drawing inferences

**EVALUATING:** making judgments; assessing

**PROBLEM SOLVING:** coming up with a way to solve a problem

**MAKING DECISIONS:** drawing conclusions in order to take action

Critical thinking skills are universal and apply to every academic discipline and vocation. Today's children may someday hold jobs that we can't yet imagine. While we can't expect to teach our kids the technical components of their eventual occupations, we *can* build thinking skills to ensure they will thrive in any environment.

# HOW TO USE THIS BOOK

The activities in this book will have children identifying problems, considering multiple perspectives, and synthesizing information to determine an outcome or make a decision. A wide variety of topics and skills are covered throughout the book. Each chapter contains real-world activities applicable to young children. Chapter by chapter, the activities increase in difficulty.

Throughout the text, young thinkers are offered hints and ways to take thinking beyond the pages of this book. As a result, you may find your child asking to construct patterns with pasta or write comparison statements about the favorite foods of family members, among other hands-on activities!

# A KID'S GUIDE TO CRITICAL THINKING

· · · · · · · · · · · · · · · · · · · · · · · · · · · · · · · · · · · · · · ·

**Hello, Thinker!**

Yes, you! You already know how to think, but you are about to become an even better thinker. Just as you can make your muscles stronger with exercise, you can make your brain stronger by practicing different types of thinking. In this book, you will practice using information to solve problems. In these pages, you will visit an amusement park, the zoo, and a school. You will play outside and throw a party. And with each activity, you will become a stronger thinker.

· · · · · · · · · · · · · · · · · · · · · · · · · · · · · · · · · · · · · · ·

**You will learn how to**

✔ **IDENTIFY:** find different things

⚙ **ANALYZE:** notice how different things relate to one another

🧠 **REASON:** draw a conclusion

🔍 **EVALUATE:** make a judgment

💡 **PROBLEM SOLVE:** think of a way to do something

🍸 **MAKE A DECISION:** take all the information you have and think of what to do next

**Let's get started!**

# Chapter 1

# GOING TO AN AMUSEMENT PARK

• • • • • • • • • • •

*Wheee!* All the activities in this chapter have to do with things you might find in an amusement park. You will get creative with cotton candy words, learn how to complete a sudoku puzzle, and design your own ride. Each activity includes a hint or a few possible answers to help you get started. The activities become more difficult as you work through the chapter. Let the fun begin!

# ACTIVITY 1: Cotton Candy Word Creation

Use the letters on each serving of cotton candy to build words, then write these words down on the next page. You may reuse sets of letters as many times as you would like. Many of the words will be something you see or could find in an amusement park.

As you try to make words from these word parts, your brain chooses which parts work together and which parts do not. It must also figure out which word parts are best placed at the start of a word and which word parts are best placed at the end of a word.

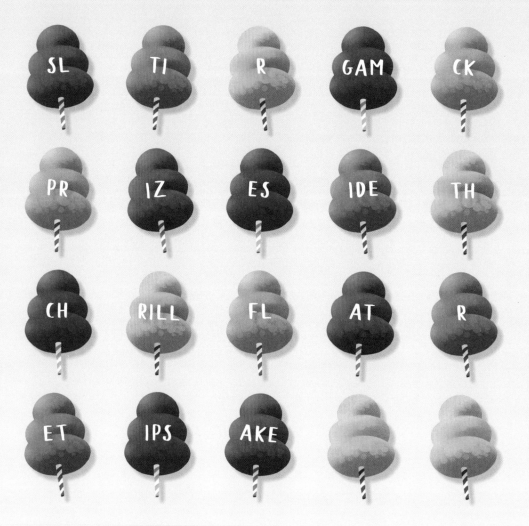

SL   TI   R   GAM   CK

PR   IZ   ES   IDE   TH

CH   RILL   FL   AT   R

ET   IPS   AKE

CHIPS
....................................    ....................................    ....................................
RAKE
....................................    ....................................    ....................................

....................................    ....................................    ....................................

....................................    ....................................    ....................................

....................................    ....................................    ....................................

....................................    ....................................    ....................................

....................................    ....................................    ....................................

....................................    ....................................    ....................................

⭐ **Challenge:** Fill in each blank cotton candy with a different word part. What additional words can you make?

....................................    ....................................    ....................................

....................................    ....................................    ....................................

....................................    ....................................    ....................................

# ACTIVITY 2:
## One of These Things Is Not Like the Others

Look at each group of words. In each group, there is one that does not match the rest. Circle the word that does not belong. When you choose things that do not belong to a group, your brain must figure out how different things are related.

| JUMP | RUN | DARTS | RING TOSS |
|---|---|---|---|
| PLAY | HOT DOG | BUMPER CARS | BALLOON |

| SNEAKERS | RUN | EXCITED | NERVOUS |
|---|---|---|---|
| SUN-GLASSES | MAP | LAUGH | THRILLED |

| CARAMEL APPLE | FUNNEL CAKE | ROLLER COASTER | TENT |
|---|---|---|---|
| CHICKEN TENDERS | CANDY BAR | SWINGS | CAROUSEL |

HINT: In the first set, *hot dog* does not belong. A hot dog is something to eat. All the other words are actions you can do in an amusement park. In the second set, *balloon* does not belong. All the other words are activities you can do in an amusement park.

⭐ **Challenge:** Write your own "which does not belong" activity using words that have to do with a trip to an amusement park.

# ACTIVITY 3: What to Ride?

A group of friends is visiting an amusement park. They have a look at the map and must decide which rides they would like to go on. Read about what each person likes to do. Write the person's name in the correct column(s). Then decide which ride everyone would like to do together.

Your brain must use reasoning to solve this problem. The chart helps you organize information so you can make a decision based on these facts.

- Hannah likes the giant slide and the merry-go-round.

- Liam likes the merry-go-round and the roller coaster.

- Kendall likes all three rides.

- Micah likes the merry-go-round.

- Rafi likes the merry-go-round and the giant slide.

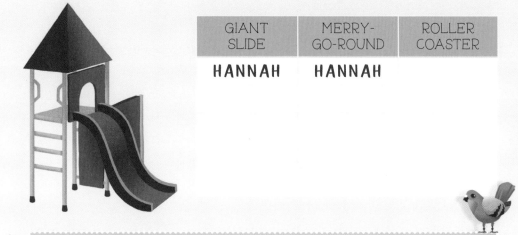

| GIANT SLIDE | MERRY-GO-ROUND | ROLLER COASTER |
|---|---|---|
| HANNAH | HANNAH | |

**HINT:** Hannah's likes have already been added to the chart. When you have entered each person's likes, the column that has everyone's name in it is the ride that everyone wants to do.

**Challenge:** Do you agree most with Hannah, Liam, Kendall, Micah, or Rafi? Think of two reasons why you agree most with that person. When you explain why, you justify your thinking with reasons.

# ACTIVITY 4: What to Buy?

Read the clues and use the Gift Shop price board on the next page to determine which items make the most sense for each person to purchase. When you read clues like this and apply them to a set of information, you are using a skill called deductive reasoning.

CLUE: Reid wants to spend exactly $4. He also wants to have something to eat and something to remember the trip by. What can he get?

.......................................    .......................................

HINT: In this case, Reid needs something that is food and something to help him remember the park. If an item costs $4 or more, he cannot have it, because he needs two things. This means he cannot have the hot dog and drink combo or the T-shirt. What is left to eat? Popcorn would take all his money. The only two items that could total exactly $4 and meet his needs are a pretzel and a postcard.

CLUE: Hayden bought a postcard, a water bottle, and something to eat. He spent $6. What did he buy to eat?

.......................................

CLUE: Yasmin brought $9 to the park. She has $0.50 left and bought only food/drink items. What did she buy?

.......................................    .......................................

CLUE: Camden and Emerson share their purchases. They bought ride tickets, two pretzels, and one other item. They spent $12. What was their other item?

.......................................

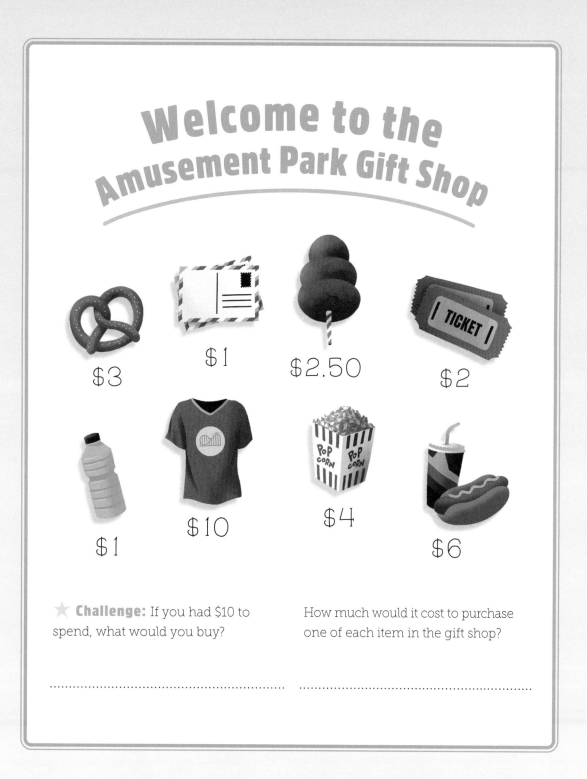

# Welcome to the Amusement Park Gift Shop

$3

$1

$2.50

$2

$1

$10

$4

$6

⭐ **Challenge:** If you had $10 to spend, what would you buy?

How much would it cost to purchase one of each item in the gift shop?

....................................................

....................................................

# ACTIVITY 5: Always, Sometimes, Never

Read the statement below. Decide if it is always true, sometimes true, or never true.

**Girls like roller coasters and boys like merry-go-rounds.**

This sentence is sometimes true. *Some* girls like roller coasters, and *some* boys like merry-go-rounds. But not *every* girl likes roller coasters, and not *every* boy likes merry-go-rounds.

Read each statement below. Circle whether it is always true, sometimes true, or never true. When you do this, you are making a judgment.

| | | | |
|---|---|---|---|
| The line to get into the park takes more than an hour to get through. | ALWAYS | SOMETIMES | NEVER |
| Cotton candy and a funnel cake make a healthy dinner. | ALWAYS | SOMETIMES | NEVER |
| Safety is important in an amusement park. | ALWAYS | SOMETIMES | NEVER |
| The roller coaster closes because of lightning. | ALWAYS | SOMETIMES | NEVER |
| People think roller coasters are the best ride in the park. | ALWAYS | SOMETIMES | NEVER |

HINT: When you work on each statement, ask yourself if there is any chance it may *not* be true. If there is, this will help you know the answer is not "always."

# ACTIVITY 6: Sudoku

This type of puzzle is called sudoku. Complete the grid so each row and each column contains each picture only one time.

When you work on sudoku puzzles, your brain must make many decisions to decide how to fit the pieces together. You look for patterns to figure out what can and cannot go in each space. This is called deductive reasoning.

# ACTIVITY 7: Build-a-Word

When you build words, your brain thinks about relationships between letters and also about which parts can be put together to make a whole. Make as many words as you can with the letters shown below. A few words are already in the chart to get you started!

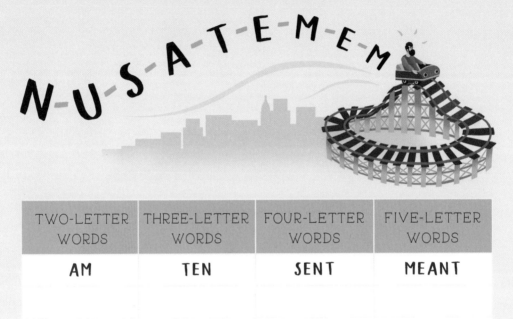

| TWO-LETTER WORDS | THREE-LETTER WORDS | FOUR-LETTER WORDS | FIVE-LETTER WORDS |
|---|---|---|---|
| AM | TEN | SENT | MEANT |
| | | | |
| | | | |
| | | | |
| | | | |

**HINT:** Start by making two-letter combinations that form a word. Then move to three-letter words, four-letter words, and five-letter words.

The word that uses all the letters is ................................................. !

# ACTIVITY 8: Design a Ride!

Amusement park designers are looking for suggestions for things kids would like to see as the newest attraction. The designers are looking for something that will entertain the whole family and be simple to construct. Use the space below to draw a picture of a new ride, and label the important parts.

When you create something from scratch, you use both critical and creative thinking. In this design challenge, you must create a ride that is easy to build *and* popular with the whole family. These details are called limits. You are limited by the fact that the ride must be easy to build. You are limited by the fact that the ride must be popular with the whole family, which includes little kids, teens, and adults.

# ACTIVITY 9: Make a Schedule

This is a challenging activity called a logic grid. Logic grids are great practice for critical thinking because you must think about multiple ideas coming together at the same time. This calls for analysis and problem solving. Both are high-level critical thinking skills.

Use the clues to complete the chart showing Maeve's plan for her morning at the amusement park.

- Maeve expects to spend 10 minutes on the giant slide and 5 minutes walking to the swings from the giant slide.

- Riding the carousel should not happen after eating anything.

- It will take 20 minutes to complete the first event.

- Maeve's grandmother gave her some money to enjoy an ice-cream cone while she is at the park, and she'll end her day on a *sweet* note.

| TIME | EVENT |
|------|-------|
| 9:00 | |
| | GIANT SLIDE |
| | |
| 10:45 | |

HINT: You will need to figure out times *and* what will be happening. Read *all* the clues before you write in the chart. See how the first clue does not match the first time listed in the chart? You can fill in the blanks in any order as you figure them out.

★ **Challenge:** Think about times when other people have designed a schedule for you. School, after-school activities, and even your meals are on some sort of schedule. If you could spend a day doing anything you wanted, what would you include? How long would you spend on each activity? Create a schedule of your dream day.

# Chapter 2

# GOING TO THE ZOO

· · · · · · · · · ·

No time to monkey around now; we are headed to the zoo! In this chapter, all the activities are related to animals and things you can see at the zoo. You will help a zookeeper unscramble a confusing situation, use clues to determine a path through the zoo, and try a new puzzle that involves math and animals. Have a roarin' good time!

# ACTIVITY 1: **Help the Zookeeper**

Welcome to the zoo! Unfortunately, there is a major problem: The animals have left their homes. They also scrambled the signs in front of their habitats. The zookeeper is not sure where to put each animal. Unscramble the animal names. Then draw a line to the correct habitat for each.

- **eabr** ..............................
- **irdb** ..............................
- **gmflaino** ..............................

- **kynome** ..............................
- **ffgiaer** ..............................

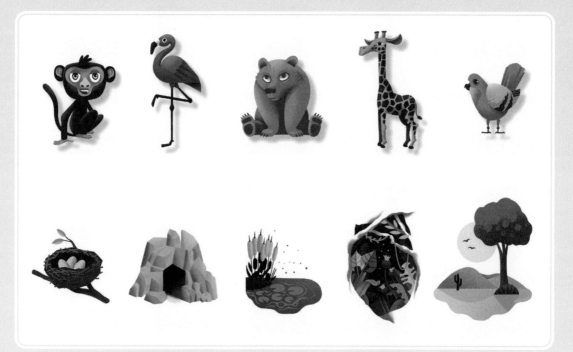

⭐ **Challenge:** Make a list of your five favorite animals. Use your list to create your own animal word scrambles. See if a family member or friend can solve them!

# ACTIVITY 2: **Sort the Animals**

Write the name of each zoo animal in the correct column of the chart.

**OWL**      **SNAKE**      **LION**      **MONKEY**

**BEAVER**      **TIGER**      **IGUANA**

| HAS FUR | CAN FLY | HAS LEGS | HAS SCALES |
| --- | --- | --- | --- |
| | | | |
| | | | |
| | | | |
| | | | |

**HINT:** Ask yourself if the animal matches the header for each column. If the answer is yes, write the animal in that column. If an animal fits in more than one group, write its name in both places.

⭐ **Challenge:** Add another animal that fits in each category.

# ACTIVITY 3: True or False?

Look at the map. Write three sentences about the map that are true. Write three sentences that are false. It is pretty easy to come up with true statements. But when you come up with false statements, you must push your brain to analyze the picture carefully and to not make adjustments to what you are looking at.

| TRUE STATEMENTS | FALSE STATEMENTS |
|---|---|
|  |  |
|  |  |
|  |  |

★ **Challenge:** Choose a zoo animal you know a lot about, such as a bear or a turtle. Write three true statements and three false statements about the animal. Ask a family member to read your statements and see if they agree with them. If there is a disagreement, look up the answer online or in an encyclopedia.

| TRUE STATEMENTS | FALSE STATEMENTS |
|---|---|
|  |  |
|  |  |
|  |  |

# Welcome to the Zoo

# ACTIVITY 4:
## Find Your Way Through the Zoo

This zoo is a big place! Use the clues to draw the path you will take through the zoo.

- You will see the flamingos first.
- After the koalas you will see the hippopotamuses.
- You will visit the monkeys before the koalas.

HINT: Read all the clues first.

★ **Challenge:** Write a clue for each animal along the path. See if a friend or family member can guess the animal's name from your clue.

# ACTIVITY 5: Choose the Categories

Sort the animals into categories you create. Do not forget to label the top of each column with a category heading! When you are finished, make a list of other types of things you could sort into categories.

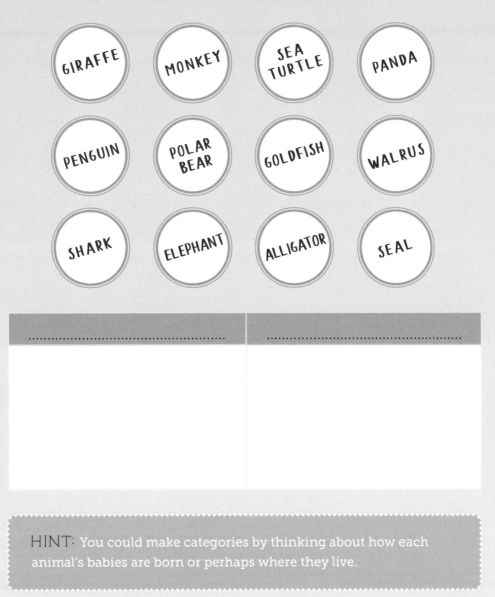

|  |  |
| --- | --- |
| | |

HINT: You could make categories by thinking about how each animal's babies are born or perhaps where they live.

# ACTIVITY 6: Zoo Sudoku

Complete the sudoku grid so each row and column contains each animal's picture just once.

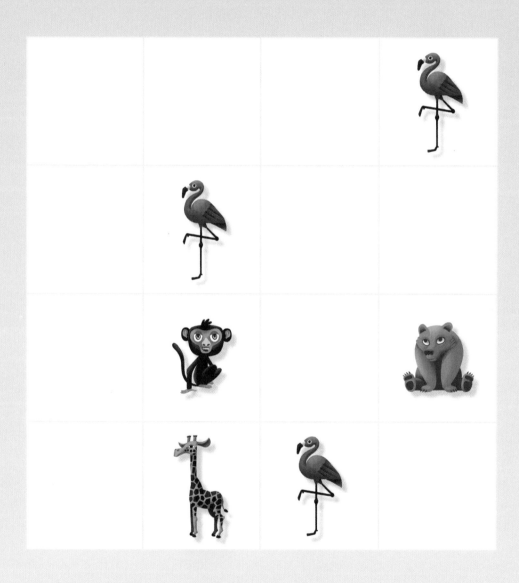

# ACTIVITY 7: Build-a-Word

Make as many words as you can with the letters shown below. They do not have to be related to a zoo.

O G T L O S O I Z

| TWO-LETTER WORDS | THREE-LETTER WORDS | FOUR-LETTER WORDS |
|---|---|---|
| TO | SIT | LOGO |
| | | |
| | | |
| | | |

HINT: Start by making two-letter combinations that form a word. Then move to three-letter words and four-letter words.

The word that uses all the letters is ...................................................... !

*(It is a person who knows a lot about animal behavior.)*

# ACTIVITY 8: Adding Animals

Each animal represents a number. Your goal is to figure out what each animal is worth in order to solve the number sentences. This is tricky! Your brain must build an understanding using many pieces of information. To do this activity, use the guess-and-check method. If the answer is too big or too small, make another guess that will get you closer to the solution.

HINT: Start with the beaver being worth 5. Work on each number sentence in the order that it appears on the page.

★ **Challenge:** Which three different animals could you add to equal 10?

..............................................

..............................................

..............................................

(beaver) + (snake) = 7

..............    ..............

(beaver) + (tiger) + (tiger) = 7

..............    ..............    ..............

(flamingo) + (snake) = 11

..............    ..............

(owl) + (squirrel) = 7

..............    ..............

(owl) + (tiger) = 5

..............    ..............

(squirrel) + (beaver) = 8

..............    ..............

(flamingo) + (beaver) = 14

..............    ..............

# ACTIVITY 9: Entertain an Animal!

Sometimes, animals can get unhappy if they do not have things to play with and make them think. A real-world challenge that a zookeeper faces is keeping animals entertained inside their enclosures.

Choose a zoo animal. Design a puzzle, a toy, or something else to add to the zoo habitat to keep this animal happy. Keep in mind that the zoo-keeper wants the animals to move as much as possible.

# Chapter 3

# GOING TO SCHOOL

· · · · · · · · ·

*Ring, ring!* Class is in session! Your hard work is really paying off! In this chapter, we will focus on school-related puzzles and activities. You'll hunt for shapes in a school scene, solve a cafeteria seating-chart dilemma, and learn how to solve a new type of puzzle called an analogy. Grab a sharp pencil (to go with your sharp brain!) and let's get started.

# ACTIVITY 1: **Shape Hunt**

Search for shapes in this picture. Look for at least **three triangles, four rectangles,** and **five things that are round.** For this activity you are identifying parts of a whole. You must notice how the shapes fit into the larger picture.

★ **Challenge:** How else can shapes be parts of a whole? Draw a picture of your favorite thing at school using only triangles, rectangles, ovals, and squares.

# ACTIVITY 2: Word Find

Grab a book or magazine and hunt for words that fit each category.

Find 3 words that end with -ent
Example: Bent

find 3 words that start with th-
Example: Thimble

Find 3 words that have double consonants in the middle
Example: Button

Find 3 words that end with -tion
Example: Attention

★ **Challenge:** Use the same book or magazine to find three adjectives. An adjective is a word that tells more about a noun. The phrase "little red shoe" has two adjectives that describe the shoe in more detail.

# ACTIVITY 3: Find the Set

In each grid, three school words go together to form a set. One word does not belong to the set. Draw a line through the word that does not belong. Then find a word or phrase that describes the common items.

In this activity, your brain will light up with multiple types of thinking! Together, these skills are called deductive reasoning. As you think about the parts of a set, your brain evaluates the options and considers what they have in common. You then deduce, or decide, which one does not belong as part of the set.

| | |
|---|---|
| PENCIL | WHITEBOARD |
| PEN | MARKER |

...................................................

| | |
|---|---|
| TEACHER | CUSTODIAN |
| PRINCIPAL | STUDENT |

...................................................

| | |
|---|---|
| ADDITION | SUBTRACTION |
| HISTORY | MULTIPLICATION |

...................................................

| | |
|---|---|
| SWIM | RIDE A BIKE |
| WALK | RIDE A BUS |

...................................................

| | |
|---|---|
| KEYBOARD | COMPUTER |
| PROJECTOR | BOOKSHELF |

...................................................

⭐ **Challenge:** Pull four school supplies out of your backpack. See what categories you can make with the items. Challenge your family to look at a set of items and figure out which one does not belong.

# ACTIVITY 4: **Analyze an Analogy**

Analogies are fun. An analogy is like a tiny puzzle inside another puzzle! To solve one, you must figure out how the first two words are related. Once you do, the puzzle becomes a piece of cake, because the second two words are related in the same way.

| **SOLVE** | **MARKER** | **GYM** | **SCISSORS** |

Use a word from the box above to complete each analogy.

- *Sing* is to *music* class as *run* is to ............................................. *class.*

- *Write* is to *pencil* as *cut* is to ............................................. .

- *Book* is to *read* as *calculator* is to ............................................. .

- *Eraser* is to *pencil* as *cap* is to ............................................. .

The next few analogies are more difficult. There is no word bank. Fill in the blank by looking at the rest of the sentence.

- *Colored pencil* is to *crayon* as ............................... is to *yardstick.*

- *Backpack* is to ............................................. as *chair* is to *sit in.*

- *Doctor* is to ............................................. as *teacher* is to *student.*

> HINT: To decide how the words are related, ask yourself these questions: Are they the same? Are they opposites? Is one a part and the other the whole? An example of a part-to-whole relationship would be *page* and *book.*

★ **Challenge:** Solve these math analogies:

*1* is to *3* as *4* is to ...............................................

*10* is to *15* as *20* is to ...............................................

# ACTIVITY 5: **Form a Category**

Sort these words into three categories. Write each category at the top of a column. In each column write the words that fit the category. Then add one more word to each category.

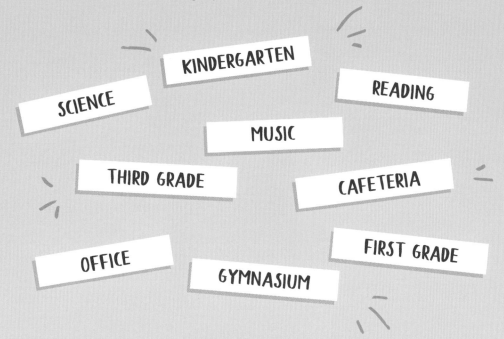

KINDERGARTEN

SCIENCE

READING

MUSIC

THIRD GRADE

CAFETERIA

OFFICE

FIRST GRADE

GYMNASIUM

| | | |
|---|---|---|
| | | |
| | | |
| | | |

# ACTIVITY 6: Making Number Sentences

Look at the numbers on each backpack. Use any combination of the numbers, plus addition or subtraction signs, to write number sentences that equal 15. You may use the addition and subtraction signs over and over, but you can only repeat a number if there is more than one of it on the backpack.

This activity exercises the problem-solving area of your brain! Changing the combination of numbers over and over until you get the result you want is challenging.

.................................... = 15         .................................... = 15

.................................... = 15         .................................... = 15

.................................... = 15         .................................... = 15

.................................... = 15         .................................... = 15

# ACTIVITY 7: **Build-a-Word**

Make as many words as you can using these letters.

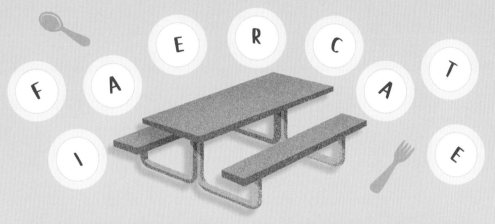

| TWO-LETTER WORDS | THREE-LETTER WORDS | FOUR-LETTER WORDS |
|---|---|---|
| IT | RAT | TEAR |
|  |  |  |
|  |  |  |
|  |  |  |
|  |  |  |

The word that uses all the letters is ...............................................!

HINT: Remember to start by making two-letter combinations that form a word. Then move to three-letter words and four-letter words.

⭐ **Challenge:** What words can you make using the letters in the word *education?* Make a chart like the one above.

# ACTIVITY 8: School Supplies Arithmetic

Each school supply stands for a number. Figure out the number value of each item.

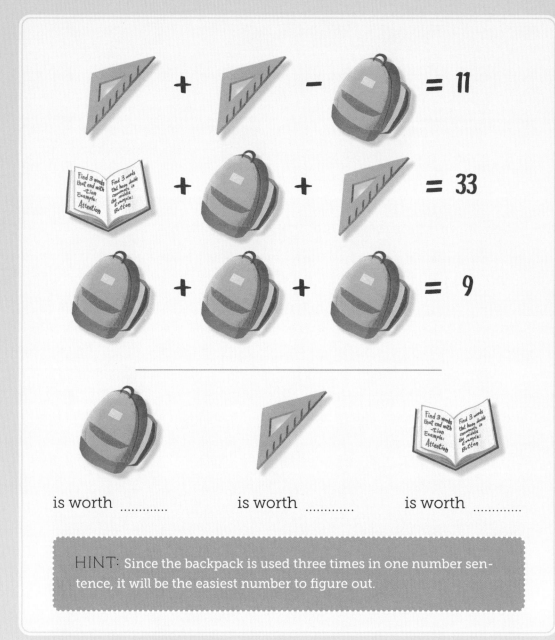

is worth ............     is worth ............     is worth ............

HINT: Since the backpack is used three times in one number sentence, it will be the easiest number to figure out.

★ **Challenge:** Assign a value to each of these school supplies: pencil, paper, and scissors. Write three of your own number sentences using these images. (Be sure to provide a number after the equals sign.) Then challenge a family member or friend to figure out what each item is worth.

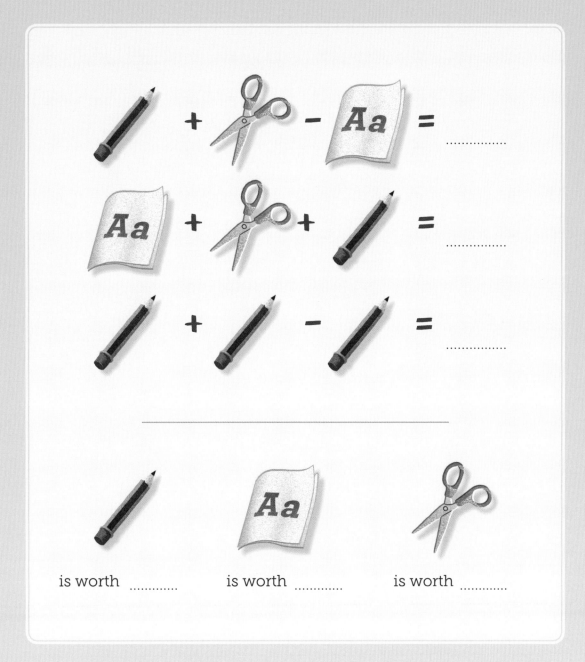

is worth ............     is worth ............     is worth ............

# ACTIVITY 9: Where Do They Sit?

A teacher has a seating chart of who sits together during lunch, but he has lost it. Students give him the following clues. It is up to you to help the teacher complete the seating chart.

1. The people whose names begin with the same letter all sit together at table 1.

2. Michelle, Kevin, and Sahara sit at different tables from each other. None of them sits at table 3.

3. Josh sits at table 3.

4. Everyone who sits at table 4 has three syllables in their name.

5. Kevin and Beto play soccer with Josh, but only two of these teammates sit together.

6. Cheyenne sits next to Beto, and Nick sits next to Kevin.

7. Nick does not sit with Ahmed, but he does sit at table 2.

8. Table 3 has two empty seats.

EMIRA
MICHAEL
MONTE
BETO
MICHELLE
KEVIN
RAFAEL
NICK
SAHARA
CHEYENNE
AHMED
MEERA
DESTINY
JOSH

HINT: Although it may not look like it, this is a logic-grid-style puzzle. And it is a tough one! Read all of the clues multiple times. You can start recording your answers in any order.

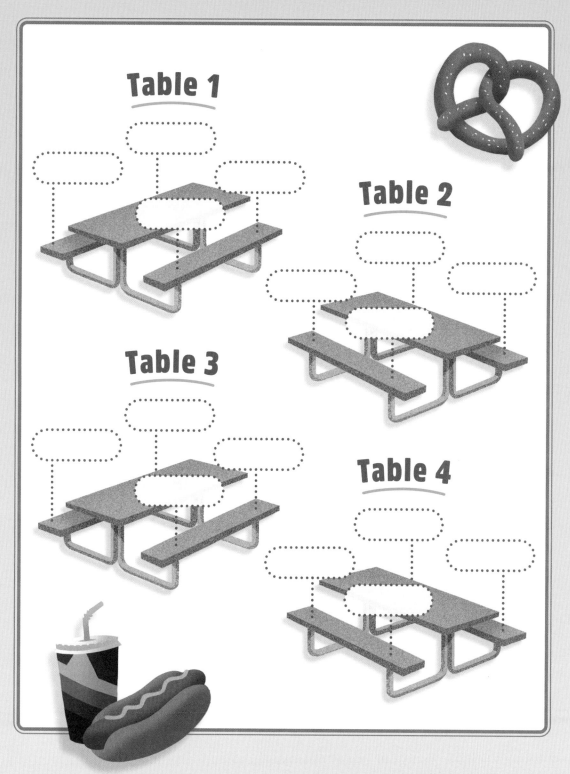

# Table 1

# Table 2

# Table 3

# Table 4

# ACTIVITY 10: Favorite Subjects

Melissa, Jason, Zhang, and Maritza have different favorite subjects. Use the clues to determine each student's favorite subject. In this activity, you can find the fourth student's favorite subject only by process of elimination. This means that after you have matched three students to their subjects, there will be only one student and one subject left.

1. Zhang likes to get lost in fantasy worlds.

2. Maritza prefers numbers to history.

3. Maritza does not like science experiments.

4. Melissa wants to know about the past.

|         | READING | MATH | HISTORY | SCIENCE |
|---------|---------|------|---------|---------|
| MELISSA |         |      |         |         |
| JASON   |         |      |         |         |
| ZHANG   |         |      |         |         |
| MARITZA |         |      |         |         |

HINT: As you solve these, use *Xs* to mark things that are incorrect. For example, if you know that Zhang is *not* the one whose favorite subject is history, put an *X* in the box where Zhang and history meet.

⭐ **Challenge:** Which subject at school is your favorite? What about your least favorite? Write a few clues to describe what you like and dislike. Do not use the names of the subjects in your clues (see clues 1 and 4 on the previous page). See if a friend can guess your favorite and least favorite subject based on your clues!

...........................................................................................................................

...........................................................................................................................

...........................................................................................................................

...........................................................................................................................

...........................................................................................................................

...........................................................................................................................

...........................................................................................................................

...........................................................................................................................

...........................................................................................................................

...........................................................................................................................

...........................................................................................................................

...........................................................................................................................

...........................................................................................................................

# ACTIVITY 11: Create a New Device

A real-world problem that teachers must solve is how to effectively set up a classroom and organize everyone's work. Design a tool that is *not* electronic that will help teachers *or* students maximize learning. This means no power cords or batteries! Your tool can be large or small, but it should be something that can be carried by a teacher or a student.

HINT: If you are stumped, think about other tools you already use, such as binders, notebooks, and pens. Can you make something that is an improvement on something that already exists?

# Chapter 4

# GOING OUTDOORS

• • • • • • • • •

Time for some fresh air and sunshine! In this chapter, we are heading to the great outdoors. You will work on your critical thinking skills by considering cause-and-effect relationships in sports, solving a logic grid puzzle about baseball positions, and analyzing a playground scene. Shine on!

# ACTIVITY 1: Scrambled Sports

Unscramble the name of each sports-related word.

oflg      ⬭..... ..... ..... .....

scerco    ..... ⬭..... ..... ..... ..... .....

abtoolfl  ..... ..... ⬭..... ..... ..... .....

tnnies    ..... ⬭..... ..... ..... ..... .....

allasbbe  ..... ..... ..... ..... ⬭..... ..... .....

wimmngis  ..... ..... ..... ..... ⬭..... ..... ..... .....

Each word above has one letter circled. Use the circled letters to form the answer to this question: What do you say at the start of a game?

..... .....      ..... ..... ..... ..... !

★ **Challenge:** Find a family calendar or to-do list and create your own word scrambles from the words on it. Circle one letter in each to create the answer to a question.

# ACTIVITY 2: This Is In-Tents!

Use the letters on each tent to create as many words as you can. You can form at least ten words from each tent.

....................................................

....................................................

....................................................

....................................................

....................................................

....................................................

....................................................

*Use this grid to make three-letter words.*

| s | r | t |
|---|---|---|
| m | a | n |
| e | l | p |

*Use this grid to make four- and five-letter words.*

| e | k | s | o |
|---|---|---|---|
| o | l | i | r |
| d | t | y | a |
| b | j | q | u |

....................................................

....................................................

....................................................

....................................................

....................................................

....................................................

....................................................

# ACTIVITY 3: **True, False, or Maybe**

Study the picture. Then read each statement. Circle whether it is true, maybe true, or false. When you do this, your brain is making a judgment.

1. The boys are on the swings.

| TRUE | MAYBE | FALSE |
|------|-------|-------|

2. It is warm outside.

| TRUE | MAYBE | FALSE |
|------|-------|-------|

3. The child with red hair is wearing a red jacket.

| TRUE | MAYBE | FALSE |
|------|-------|-------|

4. It is October.

| TRUE | MAYBE | FALSE |
|------|-------|-------|

5. The boys are friends.

| TRUE | MAYBE | FALSE |
|------|-------|-------|

6. There is a dog in the park.

| TRUE | MAYBE | FALSE |
|------|-------|-------|

7. It is going to rain soon.

| TRUE | MAYBE | FALSE |
|------|-------|-------|

# ACTIVITY 4: Sports Cause and Effect

Every sport is based on cause-and-effect relationships. Finding these relationships makes your brain think logically and use sequencing skills. Sequencing is putting events in the order that they happened.

The first column lists events that happened during a game. The second column is what happened as a result. Draw a line to match the cause with its effect.

| CAUSE | EFFECT |
| --- | --- |
| Alajah hit a home run! | A string broke. |
| The quarterback threw the football straight and to the correct spot. | The receiver caught it and was able to score a touchdown. |
| The referee blew a whistle. | Each player already on a base scored. |
| Zander hit a tennis ball very hard with a racket that had sat in the sun for a long time. | Everyone stopped playing. |

★ **Challenge:** Take outdoors any game-playing object (ball, racket, etc.). How many cause-and-effect relationships can you create using that object, your body, and the space around you?

# ACTIVITY 5: **Race to the Finish!**

Four friends ran a race. Use the clues to determine who came in first, second, third, and fourth place, and write your answers in the white spaces below.

When you solve puzzles like this, your brain puts pieces of information together step by step, like it is building a staircase. This is called synthesizing information. With each fact, you learn a bit more to help you build the set of "stairs." Your understanding of the situation changes as you add more layers to your steps. When you have all the names in the correct spots, all the steps are connected.

- Avi is slower than Marisol.

- Avi is faster than Enzo.

- Marisol is slower than Derek.

HINT: To solve this, first figure out where Marisol's name goes. Then write the other children's names above and below her as you figure out where each one goes.

# ACTIVITY 6: Comparison Conundrums

A conundrum is a difficult problem or situation. In this activity, you'll read a sentence and choose the item on the list that best matches the sentence.

CLUE: **Circle the object that is the smallest. Put a check mark next to the object that is largest.**

- Seashell
- Beach towel
- Swim fin
- Flip-flop

CLUE: **Circle the object that is round. Put a check mark next to the object that is longest.**

- Basketball
- Baseball glove
- Tennis racket
- Soccer goal

CLUE: **Circle the object that would be least cold. Put a check mark next to the object that is the most cold.**

- Mug of cocoa
- Campfire
- Lake
- Ice cube

CLUE: **Circle the object that is most likely to be found in a park. Put a check mark next to the object that is least likely to be found in a park.**

- Flowers
- Dump truck
- Buried treasure
- Television

★ **Challenge:** Write your own clues that use adjectives to describe outdoor activities. See if a family member or friend can make the right choices.

CLUE: ..............................................................................................................................

..............................................................................................................................

- •                  • 
- •                  • 

CLUE: ..............................................................................................................................

..............................................................................................................................

- •                  • 
- •                  • 

CLUE: ..............................................................................................................................

..............................................................................................................................

- •                  • 
- •                  •

# ACTIVITY 7: Always, Sometimes, Never

You are becoming an expert at thinking carefully about different situations and how they may sometimes be true. Read each statement. Circle whether it is always, sometimes, or never true.

| | | | |
|---|---|---|---|
| 1. Soccer can only be played on a team. | ALWAYS | SOMETIMES | NEVER |
| 2. Exercise helps your body stay healthy. | ALWAYS | SOMETIMES | NEVER |
| 3. All boys like tennis and all girls like soccer. | ALWAYS | SOMETIMES | NEVER |
| 4. Baseball is a spring activity. | ALWAYS | SOMETIMES | NEVER |
| 5. Girls wear purple jerseys. | ALWAYS | SOMETIMES | NEVER |
| 6. Some sports can only be played with snow. | ALWAYS | SOMETIMES | NEVER |

★ **Challenge:** Rewrite each "always true" and "sometimes true" sentence so that it is *never* true.

................................................................................

................................................................................

................................................................................

................................................................................

................................................................................

................................................................................

# ACTIVITY 8: Outdoor Math

Each outdoor object represents a number. To do this activity, use the guess-and-check method. If the answer is too big or too small, make another guess that will get you closer to the solution.

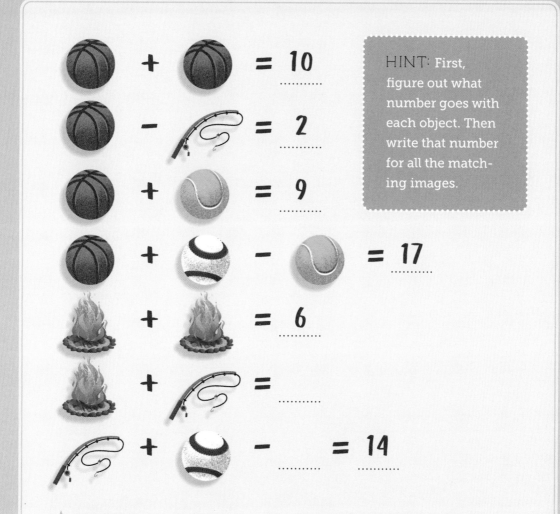

HINT: First, figure out what number goes with each object. Then write that number for all the matching images.

⭐ **Challenge:** Is it possible to combine 5 images to make a total greater than 50? Is it possible to combine 5 images to make a total greater than 100? Explain how you know.

# ACTIVITY 9: What Is My Position?

Grace, Mia, Tony, and Krey are on the same baseball team. Each is a very successful player at their position. Use the clues to determine who plays which position.

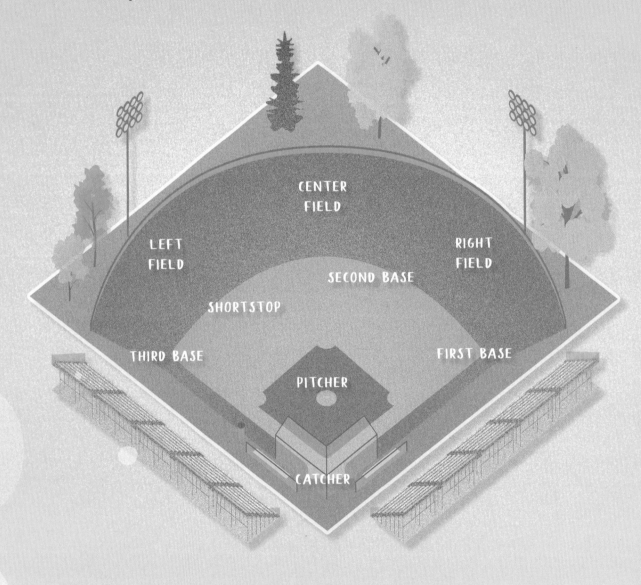

# CLUES:

1. Grace, who is not the first baseman, stands the farthest away from the catcher.

2. The shortstop and Krey carpool to baseball practice together.

3. Mia is not the first baseman, and Tony is not the catcher.

4. The catcher and Grace practiced a bit extra after they both dropped balls during the last game.

5. Krey is the catcher.

|  | FIRST BASE | SHORTSTOP | CATCHER | RIGHT FIELDER |
|---|---|---|---|---|
| GRACE |  |  |  |  |
| MIA |  |  |  |  |
| TONY |  |  |  |  |
| KREY |  |  |  |  |

# ACTIVITY 10: Complete the Grid

Draw a tent, fishing rod, or basketball in each box so every row and column of the grid has just one of each item.

# ACTIVITY 11: Create an Invention

When you spend a lot of time outside, your body adapts to the temperature of the air around you. This is why you get cold after playing in the snow and hot and sweaty in the summer heat! Invent a product that could help maintain your body temperature. It can be something to keep you cool in the summer or warm in the winter.

You can be as creative as you would like. Electronics are allowed. There is one important limit: you may use only four different materials in construction. Examples of materials are fabric and wood. Label each material as you draw your invention.

# Chapter 5

# GOING TO A PARTY

• • • • • • • • • • •

Party time! In this chapter, you will flex your critical thinking muscles with activities related to all kinds of celebrations. You will try a few new challenges, including continuing patterns, sequencing steps in a process, and balancing scales. Remember to read the directions and clues carefully. Let's stretch your thinking muscles!

# ACTIVITY 1: Rhyming Words

Look at the word in the left-hand column. Think of a word that rhymes with it that names something you might find at a party. Write the party word in the space provided. If you can think of more than one word, great!

In this activity, your brain is working hard to change just one part of each word at a time. This is great practice for "zooming in" on parts of a whole.

| | SOMETHING YOU MIGHT FIND AT A PARTY |
|---|---|
| RAKE | |
| GONG | |
| LIDS | |
| FLAGS | |
| HANDLES | |
| PLEASANT | |
| SANDY | |
| FLAMES | |
| GATES | |

HINT: Start at the beginning of the alphabet and replace the first sound in the given word with a sound from the alphabet. Move through the alphabet in this way until you find a word related to parties.

# ACTIVITY 2: Sequence of Events

Here are the steps a baker used to prepare a birthday cake. Number them 1 through 6. Number 1 is the event that happened first. Number 6 is the event that happened last. When you do this, your brain must evaluate each step and then use logical reasoning to decide how they fit together.

......... The cake is baked.

......... The cake is served.

......... Candles are added to the cake.

......... Eggs are cracked and mixed with sugar and flour.

......... Icing is added to the cake.

......... The baker pulls a mixing bowl out of the cabinet.

HINT: Ask yourself questions such as, "Can I put icing on a cake before I bake it?" If you get stuck, try reading the steps that you do have in order, then read a possible next step. If it does not make sense, try another!

⭐ **Challenge:** Write six steps for creating your favorite treat that you eat at a celebration. What would happen if you forgot to do step number 4?

# ACTIVITY 3: Last One On

Four people are waiting for a bus. They will ride to a celebration downtown. Use the clues to figure out who will get on the bus first, second, third, and last. Read *all* the clues before starting.

As you put the pieces of information together, your brain will make a mental picture of the people. Making a mental picture is called visualization. Visualization can be really helpful in solving puzzles like this. You may want to draw stick figures on the page as you determine the order.

CLUE: **Everyone else was sitting down when the man in a suit got on board.**

CLUE: **The child boarded before anyone else.**

CLUE: **The woman did not get on second.**

| | ANSWERS |
|---|---|
| This person got on the bus first. | |
| This person got on the bus second. | |
| This person got on the bus third. | |
| This person got on the bus last. | |

HINT: There is no clue about when the teen got on the bus. You will figure this out based on the process of elimination. This means you place everyone else in order, and the teen must go in the remaining spot.

# ACTIVITY 4: Birthday Gifts!

In this activity you must stretch your creative thinking skills a bit. You have four gifts, and you have no idea what is inside each package. The only things you know about the items inside are the clues listed below. Make a list of things that could possibly be in each package. Be sure your ideas fit the clues!

**The item inside Gift 1 is purple, heavy, and not round.**

GIFT 1 COULD BE:

...................................    ...................................    ...................................

**The item inside Gift 2 is long and thin, and is used indoors.**

GIFT 2 COULD BE:

...................................    ...................................    ...................................

**The item inside Gift 3 is something adored by children but not often used by adults.**

GIFT 3 COULD BE:

...................................    ...................................    ...................................

**The item inside Gift 4 is metal and comes in many varieties.** *Varieties* means "different forms."

GIFT 4 COULD BE:

...................................    ...................................    ...................................

# ACTIVITY 5: Would You Rather?

Read each question. Think carefully about what it asks. Then circle the part of the sentence that states which choice you would like better. To do this, your brain must think about the pros and cons of each option.

1. Would you rather have a small birthday gathering with just a few close friends or a big party where you include many people?

2. Would you rather have soda and vegetables, or water and ice cream, at your birthday party?

3. Would you rather get a book or an outdoor toy for a gift?

4. Would you rather *watch* a movie with your friends or *make* a movie with your friends?

5. Would you rather mail a thank-you note for each gift or hand-deliver a thank-you note for each gift?

# ACTIVITY 6: **Party Patterns**

Determine the pattern. To do this, notice what is at the beginning of the pattern, and determine how often each section is repeated. When you see a blank line, draw the missing party item. To do this, your brain takes in information about what it sees and then draws a conclusion about what comes next. There are many kinds of patterns. When you skip-count, you practice a numerical pattern!

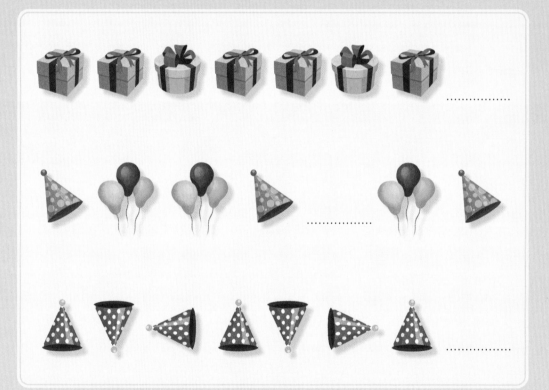

⭐ **Challenge:** Make some patterns with items around the house! Pasta shapes are great pattern-making items, and so are beads! Ask a family member to help you find some small items to use.

# ACTIVITY 7: Celebration Sudoku

Complete the celebration symbol sudoku. Each symbol must appear just once in each row. The symbols that are already placed cannot be moved.

# ACTIVITY 8: Balancing Act

To balance each scale below, both sides must weigh exactly the same. What needs to be added to the *second* scale to make each side weigh the same?

This scale is also balanced. What needs to be put on the *right* side of the second scale to make each side weigh the same?

★ **Challenge:** Make a balance puzzle of your own. You could use the same images, or use some of your favorite things instead!

Use this:                                        To help solve this:

# ACTIVITY 9: Celebrate Words

Make as many words as you can with the letters shown below. But because you are now an expert at building words, no two-letter words this time!

| THREE-LETTER WORDS | FOUR-LETTER WORDS | FIVE-LETTER WORDS |
|---|---|---|
| SKI | WIRE | FORKS |
| | | |
| | | |
| | | |
| | | |

The ultimate challenge word that uses all the letters is .................................!

★ **Challenge:** Write a clue for each word you created. Then read the clue aloud to a family member and see if they can guess the word. Give your person time to think. Do not rush them!

# ACTIVITY 10: Party Plan

Your class is having a fall party. The students will be split into three groups. Each group will move through all the activities for the party. Just one group at a time may be part of an activity.

The teacher needs your help to make the schedule. Use the clues to fill in the chart. Use an **E** for "eat pumpkin pie." Use a **W** for "watch a scary movie." Use a **B** for "bob for apples."

**Group 1** will bob for apples first.

**Group 2** will bob for apples after Group 3 does.

**Group 3** will watch the movie before anything else.

| | 1:00 – 1:30 | 1:30 – 2:00 | 2:00 – 2:30 |
|---|---|---|---|
| GROUP 1 | | E | W |
| GROUP 2 | E | | |
| GROUP 3 | | | E |

HINT: Read all the clues first. If you get stumped, start with the last clue and read *up* the list.

# ACTIVITY 11: Adding to the Calendar

Desserts are a staple at celebrations across the globe. Birthday parties, religious celebrations, and other family gatherings often include sweet treats. For this challenge, you have a problem to solve and an opportunity to be creative.

There are not many holidays celebrated during the month of August. First, create a holiday that could be celebrated during the month of August. Second, design a dessert that should be served at your holiday celebration. The dessert should match the theme of the holiday. One more thing: Your dessert should not be the same as a dessert your family enjoys for another holiday.

HINT: Use your imagination! To make your dessert, think of flavors that go well together but are not featured in other common desserts. For example, peanut butter and pretzels mixed together in ice cream . . . yum!

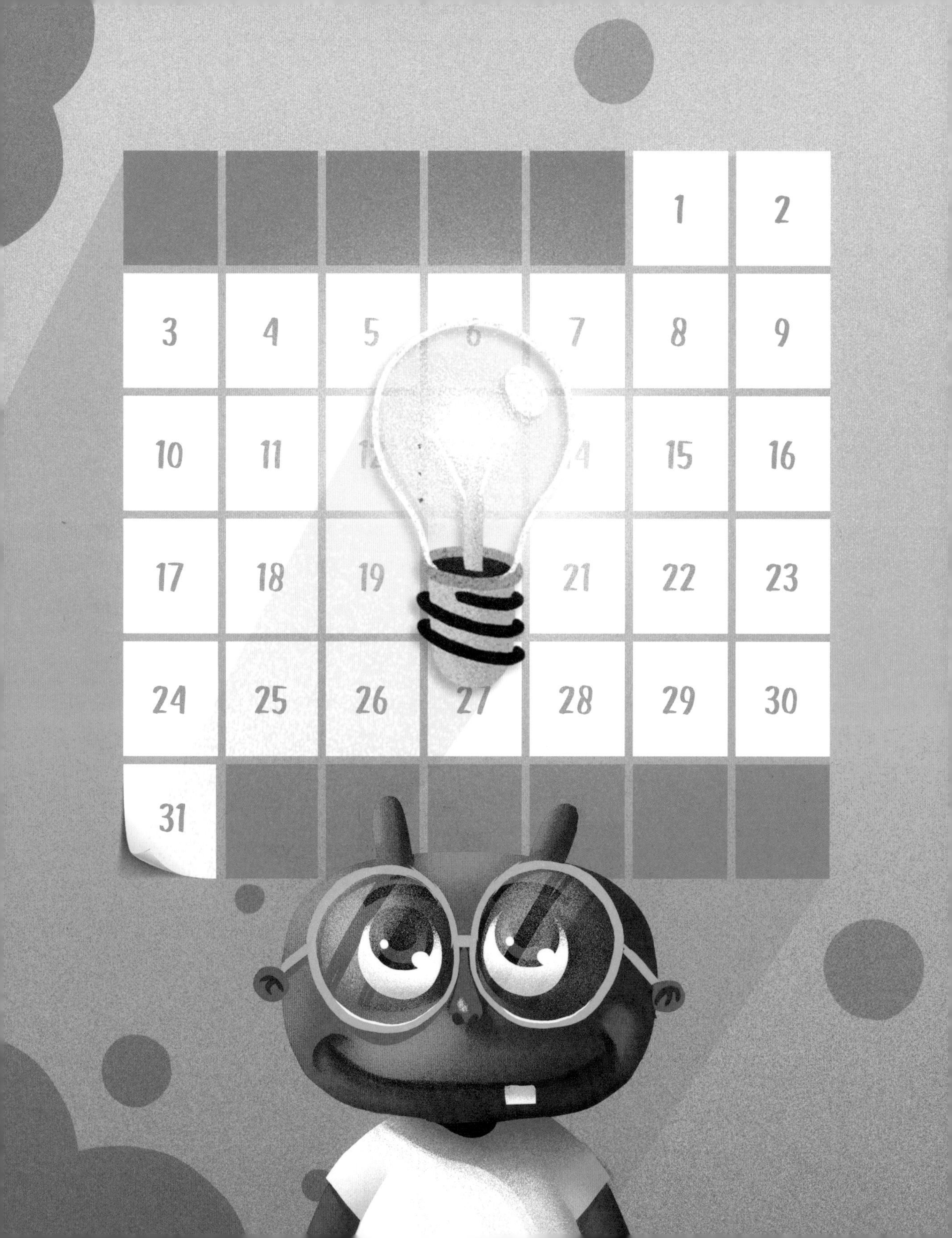
1
2
3
4
5
6
7
8
9
10
11
15
16
17
18
19
21
22
23
24
25
26
27
28
29
30
31

# Chapter 6

# USING CRITICAL THINKING EVERY DAY

• • • • • • • • • • •

Congratulations, young thinker! You have tackled a variety of activities, from finding patterns to building words and solving logic grids. As you worked on these activities, you exercised your brain. It grew stronger. Better yet, you developed important skills you will use every day of your whole life!

At the start of the book, you read that you would use six critical thinking skills. You used those six skills on the activities throughout the book. Often you used more than one type of thinking on an activity. Now let's look at how those skills work together in real life.

Here are several different scenarios that may happen in your life. A scenario is an event or a pretend scene. Picture yourself as the main character in each scene.

### YOUR FRIEND SAYS SOMETHING UNKIND ABOUT A CLASSMATE. YOU KNOW IT IS NOT TRUE.

You evaluated your friend's statement to know that it is false. Consider why your friend might be spreading lies. Does your friend benefit from this lie? Is your friend usually unkind to others? Now think about possible ways to react. Will you nod your head? Will you repeat the unkind comment? Or will you stand up for your classmate? Will you tell how you know the statement is not true? Will you stay friends? If the situation is serious, you may have to choose to get an adult involved.

### AT THE TOY STORE, YOU MUST CHOOSE BETWEEN TWO GAMES. ONE IS A VIDEO GAME, AND ONE IS AN OUTDOOR GAME. YOU CAN BUY ONLY ONE.

In this case, you have two really good options! Identify the differences between them. Does one encourage healthy habits more than the other? Do you have a friend who has the game already, and you could play using their game? Or do you need your own version of the game to play with your friends? Your brain will continue to identify details about each, and you will evaluate how much those details matter to you. Eventually, after careful consideration, you make a final decision.

### HOW CAN YOU CONVINCE AN ADULT TO GIVE $50 TO A CHARITY YOU FEEL STRONGLY ABOUT?

First, identify what makes your cause worthwhile. Does it help animals in need? Provide books for kids who do not have books to read? Then consider the feelings of the person you want to ask to donate money. Is there something that this person and your charity have in common? For example, is the person you are talking to an animal lover?

Pointing out commonalities, or things that are the same, can be helpful when you want to convince someone to feel positively about something. You can also explain how this donation will help the charity solve problems. In this case, you will not be the one making the decision. However, your reasoning skills will hopefully help someone else make a decision you feel great about!

## IT IS THE CHAMPIONSHIP GAME AGAINST YOUR BIGGEST RIVAL, AND YOU HAVE TO MAKE THE NEXT PLAY.

Throughout the game, you have constantly noticed the other team's moves and strategies for scoring. You have responded in a way that stopped them from scoring too much!

Now you have to put that information in your head and combine it with what you know *you* can do well. This is synthesizing: taking parts of different pieces of information and combining them with what you already know. The decision you make on which play to use may make or break the game. Think before you act!

## YOUR SCIENCE CLASS IS DESIGNING AN EXPERIMENT TO SEE HOW VINEGAR, BAKING SODA, AND SALT WORK TOGETHER.

You may have learned about each ingredient separately. Is it a solid or a liquid? What color is it? What is its texture? When you learned those things, you were identifying details. Now you are going to use all the information you know to make a hypothesis, which is an educated guess.

Your hypothesis will be about what *might* happen when all the ingredients are combined. Then decide how to combine the ingredients. How much of each should you use? What should you add first? Second?

When you visualize doing the experiment, what do you picture happening when you mix the ingredients together? What might change if you did the experiment differently? When you work through the scientific method, you utilize all six of the critical thinking skills.

## YOUR PARENTS HAVE SAID THEY WILL CONSIDER ADDING A PET TO YOUR FAMILY, IF YOU CAN PROVE THAT YOU ARE RESPONSIBLE ENOUGH TO TAKE CARE OF IT.

This scenario is similar to the charity scenario, except this time, you are thinking of details about yourself. What proof can you offer your parents that shows that you can be responsible? Think about how often you follow through with something you say you will do. Do you always, sometimes, or never follow through?

Evaluate your previous actions and think through how you can use them as examples of being responsible. If you need to change your actions, analyze how you can improve. Do you make your bed on weekends but never weekdays? Do you start to unload the dishwasher and then walk away with the task half-finished?

When you evaluate and analyze your actions, you may see things from your parents' perspective. You can also make a plan about how to act more responsible . . . and maybe earn that pet!

## ALL SUMMER, YOU HAVE WORKED TO DO EXTRA CHORES FOR ALLOWANCE MONEY. IT IS TIME TO DECIDE HOW TO SPEND (OR SAVE) IT.

As summer winds down, you may want to spend your money on new school supplies or fancy socks for the first day back to school. It is your money. So it is up to you to consider the positives and negatives of all your options. Do not forget that you could also save your money for something that costs more that you would like to buy in the future.

What are the positives of spending your money on new school supplies? Are there any negatives to spending all your money on a new pair of really cool striped socks? How might you feel in the future about the decision you made?

Spending money requires a lot of evaluating. Let's say you decide to buy the fancy socks. You must think about the similarities and differences between options. Do you want the blue-striped socks or the orange-striped ones? Why? Other people's opinions might affect your choice, too.

In your daily life, you can find many more scenarios like these. The next time you are faced with making a choice, no matter how small it may seem, stop for a minute. Use your critical thinking toolbox. Sometimes, taking a step back to identify and analyze details will help you consider your choices in a new way.

*Happy thinking!*

# Answer Key

## Chapter 1: Going to an Amusement Park

### ACTIVITY 1: Cotton Candy Word Creation
Possible words include: **slide, ride, ticket, prizes, games, thrill, chat, flake, flips, rake,** etc.

### ACTIVITY 2: One of These Things Is Not Like the Others
These words do not belong in the groups: **run, laugh, chicken tenders,** and **tent.**

### ACTIVITY 3: What to Ride?

| GIANT SLIDE | MERRY-GO-ROUND | ROLLER COASTER |
|---|---|---|
| HANNAH KENDALL RAFI | HANNAH LIAM KENDALL MICAH RAFI | LIAM KENDALL |

### ACTIVITY 4: What to Buy?
Hayden bought popcorn.
Yasmin bought cotton candy and the hot dog/drink combo.
Camden and Emerson's additional item was popcorn.

## ACTIVITY 5: **Always, Sometimes, Never**

Sometimes, never, always, sometimes, sometimes

## ACTIVITY 6: **Sudoku**

| POPCORN | ROLLER COASTER | T-SHIRT | COTTON CANDY |
|---|---|---|---|
| COTTON CANDY | T-SHIRT | ROLLER COASTER | POPCORN |
| T-SHIRT | POPCORN | COTTON CANDY | ROLLER COASTER |
| ROLLER COASTER | COTTON CANDY | POPCORN | T-SHIRT |

## ACTIVITY 7: **Build-a-Word**

Here are some words that can be built: **am, us, use, men, ten, sent, mums, tease, teens, tunes,** etc. The word that uses all the letters is **amusement.**

## ACTIVITY 8: **Design a Ride!**

Answers will vary.

## ACTIVITY 9: **Make a Schedule**

9:00 carousel, 9:20 giant slide, 9:35 swings, 10:45 ice cream

# Chapter 2: Going to the Zoo

## ACTIVITY 1: Help the Zookeeper

bear          monkey
bird           giraffe
flamingo

A bear lives in a cave.         A giraffe lives in the grassland.
A monkey lives in the jungle.   A flamingo lives in water.
A bird lives in a nest.

## ACTIVITY 2: Sort the Animals

| HAS FUR | CAN FLY | HAS LEGS | HAS SCALES |
|---|---|---|---|
| BEAVER | OWL | BEAVER | SNAKE |
| TIGER | | TIGER | IGUANA |
| LION | | LION | |
| MONKEY | | MONKEY | |
| | | IGUANA | |
| | | OWL | |

## ACTIVITY 3: True or False

Answers will vary.

## ACTIVITY 4:
## Find Your Way Through the Zoo

First: flamingos
Second: monkeys
Third: koalas
Fourth: hippopotamuses

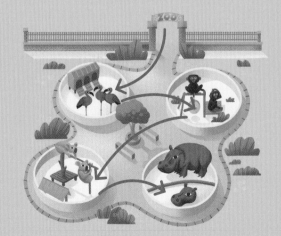

## ACTIVITY 5: **Choose the Categories**

Answers will vary based on the categories the child chooses; one potential set of categories is shown below.

| LAYS EGGS | DOES NOT LAY EGGS |
|-----------|-------------------|
| PENGUIN | POLAR BEAR |
| ALLIGATOR | ELEPHANT |
| SEA TURTLE | GIRAFFE |
| GOLDFISH | SEAL |
| | SHARK |
| | PANDA |
| | MONKEY |
| | WALRUS |

## ACTIVITY 6: **Zoo Sudoku**

| | | | |
|---|---|---|---|
| GIRAFFE | BEAR | MONKEY | FLAMINGO |
| MONKEY | FLAMINGO | BEAR | GIRAFFE |
| FLAMINGO | MONKEY | GIRAFFE | BEAR |
| BEAR | GIRAFFE | FLAMINGO | MONKEY |

## ACTIVITY 7: **Build-a-Word**

Answers will vary. Here are some words that can be built: **it, so, zig, zoo, log, tool, soil,** etc. The word that uses all the letters is **zoologist.**

## ACTIVITY 8: **Adding Animals**

beaver = 5, snake = 2, tiger = 1, owl = 4, iguana = 3, flamingo = 9
Challenge answers: beaver, snake, and iguana

## ACTIVITY 9: **Entertain an Animal!**

Answers will vary.

# Chapter 3: Going to School

## ACTIVITY 1: **Shape Hunt**

Answers will vary.

## ACTIVITY 2: Word Find
Answers will vary.

## ACTIVITY 3: Find the Set
Set name: things you write with; **whiteboard** does not belong. Set name: adults at school; **student** does not belong. Set name: math operations; **history** does not belong. Set name: ways to get to school; **swim** does not belong. Set name: electronic school tools; **bookshelf** does not belong.

## ACTIVITY 4: Analyze an Analogy
*Sing* is to *music class* as *run* is to **gym** *class.*
*Write* is to *pencil* as *cut* is to **scissors.**
*Book* is to *read* as *calculator* is to **solve.**
*Eraser* is to *pencil* as *cap* is to **marker.**
*Colored pencil* is to *crayon* as **ruler** is to *yardstick.*
*Backpack* is to **wear** as *chair* is to *sit in.*
*Doctor* is to **patient** as *teacher* is to *student.*
*1* is to *3* as *4* is to **6**          *10* is to *15* as *20* is to **25**

## ACTIVITY 5: Form a Category

| PLACES | SCHOOL SUBJECTS | GRADE LEVELS/ CLASSROOMS |
|---|---|---|
| CAFETERIA | READING | FIRST GRADE |
| OFFICE | SCIENCE | THIRD GRADE |
| GYMNASIUM | MUSIC | KINDERGARTEN |

## ACTIVITY 6: Making Number Sentences
Answers will vary. Here are some possible number sentences.
First backpack: $5 + 9 + 1 = 15$; $13 + 3 - 1 = 15$; $11 + 5 - 1 = 15$
Second backpack: $4 + 5 + 6 = 15$; $2 + 6 + 7 = 15$; $7 + 8 + 9 - 5 - 4 = 15$
Third backpack: $5 + 5 + 5 = 15$; $3 + 3 + 5 + 5 - 1 = 15$

## ACTIVITY 7: **Build-a-Word**

Answers will vary. Here are some words that can be built: **if, ice, rat, tea, feet, fear, tear,** etc. The word that uses all the letters is **cafeteria.**

## ACTIVITY 8: **School Supplies Arithmetic**

backpack = 3, triangular ruler = 7, book = 23

## ACTIVITY 9: **Where Do They Sit?**

Table 1: Michael, Meera, Michelle, Monte
Table 2: Nick, Kevin, Cheyenne, Beto
Table 3: Josh, Ahmed
Table 4: Emira, Rafael, Sahara, Destiny

## ACTIVITY 10: **Favorite Subjects**

|         | READING | MATH | HISTORY | SCIENCE |
|---------|---------|------|---------|---------|
| MELISSA | X       | X    | O       | X       |
| JASON   | X       | X    | X       | O       |
| ZHANG   | O       | X    | X       | X       |
| MARITZA | X       | O    | X       | X       |

## ACTIVITY 11: **Create a New Device**

Answers will vary.

# Chapter 4: Going Outdoors

## ACTIVITY 1: **Scrambled Sports**

Golf, soccer, football, tennis, baseball, swimming. Go team!

## ACTIVITY 2: **This Is In-Tents!**

Answers will vary. Tent 1 may include: **tan, sat, map, met, rat, rap, lap, pal, net, nap.** Tent 2 may include: **quit, took, look, book, joke, load, toad, road, kite, read, ready.**

## ACTIVITY 3: **True, False, or Maybe**

1. The boys are on the swings: true
2. It is warm outside: maybe
3. The child with red hair is wearing a red jacket: false
4. It is October: maybe
5. The boys are friends: maybe
6. There is a dog in the park: false
7. It is going to rain soon: maybe

## ACTIVITY 4: **Sports Cause and Effect**

- Alajah hit a home run, <-> so each player already on a base scored.

- The quarterback threw the football straight and to the correct spot, <-> so the receiver caught it and was able to score a touchdown.

- The referee blew a whistle, <-> so play stopped.

- Zander hit a tennis ball very hard with a racket that had sat in the sun for a long time, <-> so a string broke.

## ACTIVITY 5: **Race to the Finish!**

Derek, Marisol, Avi, Enzo.

## ACTIVITY 6: **Comparison Conundrums**

Set 1: A flip-flop is the smallest and a beach towel is the largest.
Set 2: A basketball is round and a soccer goal is the longest.
Set 3: A campfire is the least cold and an ice cube is the most cold.
Set 4: Flowers are most likely to be found in a park, and a television is least likely to be found in a park.

## ACTIVITY 7: Always, Sometimes, Never

Never, always, never, sometimes, sometimes, always

## ACTIVITY 8: Outdoor Math

basketball = 5; fishing rod = 3; campfire = 3; baseball = 6; tennis ball = 6
Fill in the blanks: campfire + fishing rod = 6; fishing rod + baseball + basketball = 14

## ACTIVITY 9: What Is My Position?

|  | FIRST BASE | SHORTSTOP | CATCHER | RIGHT FIELDER |
|---|---|---|---|---|
| GRACE | X | X | X | O |
| MIA | X | O | X | X |
| TONY | O | X | X | X |
| KREY | X | X | O | X |

## ACTIVITY 10: Complete the Grid

| FISHING ROD | TENT | BASKET-BALL |
|---|---|---|
| TENT | BASKET-BALL | FISHING ROD |
| BASKET-BALL | FISHING ROD | TENT |

## ACTIVITY 11: Create an Invention

Answers will vary.

# Chapter 5: Going to a Party

## ACTIVITY 1: Rhyming Words
Cake, song, kids, bags, candles, present, candy, games, mates/plates

## ACTIVITY 2: Sequence of Events
1. The baker pulls a mixing bowl out of the cabinet.
2. Eggs are cracked and mixed with sugar and flour.
3. The cake is baked.
4. Icing is added to the cake.
5. Candles are added to the cake.
6. The cake is served.

## ACTIVITY 3: Last One On
First: child
Second: teen
Third: woman
Fourth: man

## ACTIVITY 4: Birthday Gifts!
Answers will vary. Here are some possibilities: gift 1: a flashlight, boots, a car; gift 2: a broom, a curtain rod, a wooden spoon; gift 3: a pacifier, a teddy bear, a new box of crayons; gift 4: a coin, a medal, a pan.

## ACTIVITY 5: Would You Rather?
Answers will vary.

## ACTIVITY 6: Party Patterns
Green present; balloons; upside-down party hat

## ACTIVITY 7: Celebration Sudoku

| | | | |
|---|---|---|---|
| CAKE | PARTY HAT | STAR | BALLOONS |
| STAR | BALLOONS | CAKE | PARTY HAT |
| PARTY HAT | CAKE | BALLOONS | STAR |
| BALLOONS | STAR | PARTY HAT | CAKE |

## ACTIVITY 8: Balancing Act

First scale: a party hat should be added.
Second scale: two cakes should be added.

## ACTIVITY 9: Celebrate Words

Answers will vary. Here are some words that can be built: **sew, for, wise, woke, rose, worse, fries,** etc. The word that uses all the letters is **fireworks.**

## ACTIVITY 10: Party Plan

| | 1:00–1:30 | 1:30–2:00 | 2:00–2:30 |
|---|---|---|---|
| GROUP 1 | B | E | W |
| GROUP 2 | E | W | B |
| GROUP 3 | W | B | E |

## ACTIVITY 11: Adding to the Calendar

Answers will vary.

# About the Author

**Taylor Lang, M.Ed.,** is a classroom teacher, gifted education specialist, and curriculum resource creator. She is passionate about STEM education, children's literature, and encouraging all kids to think critically and creatively. You can connect with her online at LearningwithMissLang.com and on Twitter: @MissLang08.